£95

Millennium's End

By the Author

Textbooks:
    The Art and Craft of Poetry
    Poet's Guide
    Living Ethics:
        Developing Values in Mass Communication
    Guide to Writing Magazine Nonfiction

Social Criticism:
    Culture's Sleeping Beauty:
        Essays on Poetry, Prejudice and Belief
    Academic Socialism:
        Merit and Morale in Higher Education

Poetry:
    The Visionary
    What We Do For Music
    Platonic Love
    After Oz
    Flight from Valhalla
    Talk

Short Stories:
    Little Dragons

Novel:
    Family Values

Millennium's End

Poems

Michael J. Bugeja

Archer Books

Copyright © 1999 by Michael J. Bugeja

All rights reserved under International and Pan-American Copyright Conventions. No part of this book may be used or reproduced in any manner whatsoever without written permission, except in the case of brief quotations embodied in critical articles or reviews.

Published in the United States by:
Archer Books
P. O. Box 1254
Santa Maria, CA 93456

First edition

Publisher's Cataloging-in-Publication Data

Bugeja, Michael J.
    Millennium's end : poems / Michael J. Bugeja.
       p.   cm.
    ISBN 0-9662299-3-2
     1. Title
    P3552.U387M55   1999
    811'.54--dc21
                                                  99-41809
                                                        CIP

Jacket photo: Digital imagery® copyright 1999 PhotoDisc, Inc.

Printed in USA

E-mail: books@archer-books.com

Web site: http://www.archer-books.com

*for Lady Borton, Patricia Lull,
and Robert and Rene Glidden*

Contents

Introduction   11

I The Realist

The End of Truth	15
The End of Civility	17
The End of Zeal	18
First Person	20
Bones	21
Articles of Insurrection	
I. Penny Press	23
II. Arms	24
III. Quarter	25
IV. Seizures	26
V. Silence	27
VI. Toxic	28
VII. Price	29
VIII. Excessive	30
IX. Loopholes	31
X. Power	32
Shooter Rules	33
Littleton	34
Confessional Poetry	35
Atheist Testimonies	37
I. Prepositions	37
II. Premonitions	38
III. Propositions	39
Sans Nature	40
Hove	41

II The Revisionist

The Revisionist: *On Original Sin*	49
The Revisionist: *On Noah's Ark*	51
The Assassin Of Assisi	52
Coccinella 7—Punctata	54
SETI Sestina	55

Evangelists, Environmentalists	57
The Entomologist	58
Cicadas in New Jersey	61
Spoon River Garland	
1. AIDS	64
2. DOMESTIC VIOLENCE	65
3. CANCER	66
4. ACADEMIC SUICIDE	67
5. DOUBLE SHOOTING	68
6. ADDICTION	69
7. HOMELESSNESS	70
8. ANGEL DUST	71
9. BYSTANDER	72
10. CHILD ABUSE	73
11. ANOREXIA	74
12. DRIVE-BY	75
13. CARJACKING	76
14. BOMBING	77
15. THE GARLAND	78
Plath at Primrose Hill	79
Death Of A War Hero	80

III The Visionary

Consciousness	86
Life's Ineffable Edge	87
First Love Poem To My Son	89
Two Sounds	90
Your Mother's Harmonica	91
My Brave Asthmatic	93
Showing the House	94
The Conifer King	96
Forty in Southeast Ohio	98
Wolf	100

The Boy Who Would Be Pope	102
The Wedding Tree	103
The Gift of Cash	104
Markers	105
Distortions	106
Quantum Bluebird	107
Assemblies of God	109
Millennium's End	110
Acknowledgments	113
About the Author	115

Introduction

Every now and then . . . there is a phrase somebody in Des Moines needs to hear.

There are a lot of phrases in *Millennium's End* that somebody needs to hear, and think about. Phrases about the homeless: "I ceased to be before I ceased to be." About an AIDS victim: "You know the cause of death but not my name." About the death of an abused child: "You end up in a place without parents . . . without arguments."

This collection of poetry includes verses that are humorous, startling, tragic, penetrating, deeply literate and amazingly simple. They're about children, alive and dead, dogs, wives, husbands, the middle-aged and the old, journalists, teachers. There's a boy who would be pope, but not for reasons of religion—or maybe so. There's an incredibly evocative piece on selling a house full of emotions and memories, and a couple of other equally incisive, lovely musings on middle age. This is but a sample of Michael Bugeja's work, and it ranges from Malta to New York, from beginnings to endings, displaying a breadth of thought and a command of language, metaphor and feeling that is rarely seen.

And that is the measure of Michael. A reporter, editor, educator and ethicist; a writer of fiction, non-fiction and poetry. A runner who gets up at 4 AM to cover 7 or 10 miles with his wolf (yes, wolf), a master cook who prepares delicious meals he barely nibbles at while others devour, a computer expert who can whip up a web page or PowerPoint presentation at an hour's notice. More importantly than all those, a kind, gentle and caring man who sees into the souls of others.

There is more, of course. Kindness and gentleness are wonderful, and one cannot be a poet without caring. But those things alone do not make a poet. There has to be a certain hardness as well, a willingness and ability to skewer with a word. Michael has a brilliantly sharp mind, full of history and philosophy and science, all of which he uses in his poetry. He is impatient with fools, intolerant of lazy minds, and angry, even outraged at the pain we inflict on each other. His poetry has an edge, and a point.

Finally, and always, Michael is a joyful man, who plunges into everything he does with all his being. Never tepid, he boils and bubbles with enthusiasm, with energy and with love. That, more than skill with words or range of education, makes this a great collection. And Michael Bugeja a great friend.

Terry Anderson

I
The Realist

The End of Truth

How strange to estrange ourselves from the word
When needed most at millennium's end,

The world gone too post-modern to denote
As nugget-gold, divine, or absolute;

So truth is relative and more defined
To suit the rival disciplines, as in

Philosophical truths of academe,
Socratic and accredited, which mean

Nothing at all, tantamount to *tabloid
Truths* or CNN's misnomer "fact·oid,"

Which Mailer knows is "void of fact" and blank
As *election-year truths* of party plank,

Newt ones with America, or *gospel
Truths* of Swaggart and half-ones of Montel,

The syndicated truths of Oprah clones
Or Limbaugh and his legions, call-in drones,

Oxymorons of truth like canned applause,
Truth in advertising, disclosure laws,

The *rhetorical truths* of MLA
So similar to Simpson's DNA

Odds of accuracy, the truth serums,
Lie detectors, untestable quantum

Ones of chaos, black hole, and superstring,
The *random truths* of Darwin or Big Bang,

The uppercase *Truths* of poem and sage,
And lowercase ones of genome and judge—

All become obscurer now but equal
To truth's opposites when no one tell

Hype from myth, rumor from mill, news from source,
Fashion from art, and fiction from science.

The End of Civility

Perhaps the end came on the telephone—
The scams and slams and operator fees—
Or easily offended 911

Dispatchers hanging up emergencies
Until the dying yield and utter, *"Please."*
Some assail celebrities, the tabloids,

A prince and princess speaking journalese
About their extra-marital exploits,
Or senators in C-Span Congresses

Addressing colleagues as distinguished friends,
And then as ignoramuses and asses.
Some blame the law for justifying ends

To rape the raped and slay the buried slain,
Or cable-watching juries in hotels,
Sequestered with forbidden notes again,

Conspiring with murderers in cells
To shop a book or close a movie deal.
CEOs take stock and then take stock

To raid a rival, pension plan, or steal
The Buddha secrets of the Dow, Nasdaq,
Claiming others do it, so why not they?

For me, the end came when a friend-professor
Condemned the tenets of *"Civility—*
Evil tool of regent and oppressor"—

And hung that sign above his pentium
In a suite with internet and windows
To the outside world, to the per diem

Rate of the rude and tenured sorrows.

The End of Zeal

Because he had it, because the inane
Inequities of the world had not yet
Penetrated his psyche, he'd attain
Wealth, status—immune to the myriad
Slurs about his brownness. He toted a pad
As reporter and then as teacher-poet,

Assessing his life in the third person.
He pondered how many trees had fallen
To make pulp for an epiphany or pun,
Deciding that his fate had been transferred
Like so much tender. God, if real, had erred.
As payment he put rapists in the pen

And accolades in gruesome elegies
To the battered and the slain. He had morals
So wrote monk-fervently with sense and ease
About campus policies and correctness.
And the clerisy honored his Brownness.
He never rested weekends or on laurels

Documenting the American panorama
At millennium's end, the idol and ideal
Falling fake as snow in a cyclorama
Whenever he sighed and shook his head.
He could not stop shaking. He felt the dread
Adrenaline douse and oxidize his zeal,

That crusade virtue empowering the soul
In whose hole even his brownness withdrew.
His life was his at last, sans God or goal,
Hung out in front of him like carrot stick
On harness rope. What makes a heretic
In academe or, more precisely, who?

Someone has taught the learnéd mob to lynch
With megabyte and phone. He felt as cursed
Now as inquisitive but did not flinch
In tasseled brownness of his cap and gown.
Does anyone hear a plea in the third person,
He wondered, *or care anymore in the first?*

First Person

I sing the politics of pigment, my brown
Skin an equatorial skin able to block
And absorb the sun, my body genetic
Pumping crusaders with light, burning them
On my ember-pebble beach as they burned
My forebears at the stake. I sing of
Survival, the warrior-blacks of the basin
Who sailed into my sunny port, welcomed
With open arms into which they dropped,
Rickety, reflecting my rays. I am still
Singing the body genetic, my long narrow
Nose a nicer funnel than the pug or flat
Proboscis of enemies in siroccos,
My short stocky trunk a perfect fit
For the gift-herds of Troy. I bring
                               down
Citadels and fjords singing the body genetic,
Man of the future whose shape is the shape
Of things to come when you raise
Your sword to the sun, lancing the sky
With your cities, shielding your lungs
From the oxides of oblivion, your eyes
From the acid rain, hoarding the harvest,
Your silos full, your feedlots foul,
My fish too mercurial now for your feasts,
Packed anyhow for the journey aboard
Your barge on the oily seas. So I sing
The body genetic sitting quiet as a sphinx
While you occupy my archipelagoes, knowing
I will rise from the pyre of your waste
To rule the earth again.

Bones

The first time I felt them
Lying on the floor of my bedroom
For some reason on my back
Running my fingertips too gently
Over my dumbbell body,

I gasped. I had ribs
And could touch them.
This was the fabled melting
Of the babyfat that happens
Without anyone knowing

Like wax candy on a sill.
The timing was perfect: summer,
Girls in the polkadot twopiece
Of yore. You could see them
Sunning like lizards on lawns,

The elegant ankles,
The bridgework of breasts,
The accordion blades of the back
That stretch and release,
Another distraction.

I looked and lost the myriad
Layers of me lean as love,
Fossil beneath, the skeletal
Remains: I had pelvis, pubic,
And I rattled when I walked.

Who knew what was happening?
Nobody called my name
As I loitered out of luck,
Life on the line. Later
I realized my country had
Bones too. Its myths,
Its families don't always
Work but boast
Perfect timing, beautiful
People with bottomless

Appetites and plenty of
Partners to go around.
Some on lawns, on floors,
Some flat on their backs
In the street melting

There in front of you.

Articles of Insurrection

I.

Penny Press

Facts fail us. Even as walls
Bulldozed to oblivion

In the lederhose-light of Berlin
Came down, the bloc free,

Faxes and fascists
Dispatched, there had to be

Lawyers brokering another
Bankruptcy, chapter eleven

Revised as Dickens revised
By the penny, word, clock.

We who stand for truth
Fall for myth, amendment:

*The pen is mightier than
The sword. Congress*

Shall make no law. We live
As lines die every minute.

II.

Arms

We tattoo the aortae of love
Near the elbow,

Wear tourniquets of sorrow
On our sleeves.

Take them up
Against seas of trouble,

Canonize their coats:
Eagle, laurel. Hawk, dove.

We hold these
Arms as children do

Napalmed in the paddies,
Heave our burden ho.

No one shall infringe
The right to keep and bear them,

To embrace as generals
Embrace upon signing a truce.

III.

Quarter

Not the arms of an escutcheon
Or the eagle of a coin

Or the orbit of a moon
Between quadrature and syzygy

But the inalienable right
In war or peace

Without consent
To evict soldiers from houses.

This does not apply
To hooch or hut on enemy soil.

Only in America
Are we kings of castles.

We quarter the homeless
In casket, car or crate,

The armories full,
The missions oh so secret.

IV.

Seizures

Love-objects, obsessions,
Possessions

As prized as gazelle,
Mounted, bepedestaled

American women
Amending the right

To be secure
In their persons, houses,

Papers, effects. However
Probable the cause

No woman shall suffer
Unreasonable searches.

Even when affirmed by
Oath or vow

Nothing shall warrant
The body being seized.

V.

Silence

We have the right to remain
Silent as a millennial tree

Nobody hears falling
In the primeval forest.

Therefore
It does not exist.

Neither shall we be tried
Twice for the same offense

When rigsful of oil spill
Killing whale, eel. Seal.

Therefore
They do not exist.

We shall not be
Witness against ourselves

Without due process
If deprived of life.

VI.

Toxic

Those who poke holes in ozone
Also have rights

To speedy trials
Providing

They understand the nature
Of the accusation.

They may confront
Plaintiffs at the place

The crime was committed,
The upper atmosphere

Where talons of eagles
Cannot reach a verdict.

So let our alibis and tropes
Become allotropes of oxygen,

Breaths of fresh air
In an otherwise foul season.

VII.

Price

We brand beef to consume it,
Bears to preserve them,

Polars on ice,
Eagles on the precipice,

Whereabouts on park maps.
Our species wear

Bracelets as in a mall
Meticulously tagged.

Someone has gone hunting
Without a license,

Someone has been bagging
Game out of season

So we are suing in Yosemite.
The people must decide

How to place a value?
How to value a place?

VIII.

Excessive

Bail is relative as time.
It suits the criminal,

Not the crime.
We may rob an S&L

With access codes
Not Uzis

As in TV episodes.
We know the news is

Bad, recessive.
Yet bail suits the suite

And may not be excessive
Levied on elite

Whose rights we retain
By attorney, writ.

They plead the bargain
And we pay for it.

IX.

Loopholes

The enumeration of these rights
As in a bill—

To maintain a way of life
At the expense of life,

To wear it on our backs
As a woman wears a stole,

To mount it on our walls
As a man mounts an elk

Put down in a copse of
Cottonwood. To clear that wood,

To zone it. To zone species
In state parks and panhandle

Humanity on reservations,
Zoos of manifest destiny—

Shall not disparage others
Retained by the people.

X.

Power

Those affected most
Least afford to lose

What's left
Out of law books:

The right to keep
The word pure

So it echoes in eons
Of quiet disregard.

Talk is not cheap
When someone pays

To tap it. The body counts
When someone has to haul it

To the paddy wagon.
Ears open.

The sound of liberty
Is a siren, an alarm.

Shooter Rules

The millimeters of your life are nine.
The caliber is larger than your age.
The drug of choice is your adrenaline.
The victim can be smaller than the gauge.

A chamber has no doors, and yet revolves.
An automatic takes a clip, not gears.
You don't show up in court. You are absolved:
A case contains propellant now, not beer.

You don't subscribe, you load a magazine.
Your bullets here have talons, not the birds.
The only nests above are submachine.
Your silencer speaks louder than your words.

Rounds go off, the cops no longer make them.
You invent the rules, but cannot break them.

Littleton

The schoolyard tolls as once the graveyard did
For trenchcoat Thomas Gray, whose madding crowd
Secured the gates of mercy. Now we heed

The cable aftermath of talking heads
Advising us to *hire more armed guards,*
To *lose illegal guns.* Bulletins bombard

The internet and cheapen the debate
About the role of Hollywood and hate
Until the circus folds the tent and goes

When coverage of Columbine plateaus
With Kosovo. The images of that
Seem similar, the eerie *"rat-tat-tat"*

Of clips accompanied by audio
Of real ones, to which we have since Waco
Grown accustomed on TV as stimulus:

Littleton will slip into unconsciousness
Of information-angst and from our minds.
We've learned to fear a future that rewinds

By click of mouse, by button of remote,
Transmitting terror live by satellite,
Though some of us remember history

When news was truth and not reality.

Confessional Poetry

He'd had it with the riffraff of the world
And riffraff had had it in perverse ways
With abducted Lakota runaways
Under the eagles and elms, spread-eagled
In the Black Hills, heart of all that can be,
Or was: *Wamaka Og'naka Icante.*

He became a cop reporter covering
Rescue parties and hated that word: *party.*
Once it meant tequila and repartee
With women under an ever-tolling
Campanile, and then meant *Independent,
Republican, Democrat.* Innocent

Parties pleading with a prosecutor
Or guilty ones confessing *I stuffed a gag
In her mouth and her body in a bag.*
More often, *Didn't do her, your honor.*
He chased ambulance. In the aftermath
He'd find party-goers bleeding to death

In panhandle honky tonks or diners,
Noting their final words: *No!* or *Please tell
So-and-so I forgive and love him still.*
He'd quote callous Nebraska killers
On death row, the serial psychopaths
And sorry molesters. Satanic youths:

In the park where he would walk with his wife,
He saw a boy embed an arrowhead
In a babysitter and, blood-spattered,
Hop upon his bicycle and huff off.
The reporter flagged down a traffic cop
Who arrested the boy at a gift shop

Buying a sympathy card. Absurd symbol.
He wrote about drive-bys and gangbangers
At block parties, innocent bystanders
Mowed down dancing. He'd follow the patrol
To document the remains of rednecks
Ramming pickup trucks into poles. At wrecks

He'd step over hooded bodies at rest
Like stones in streams, to reach the other side.
He wrote the obit when his father died
Because editors said he knew him best.
Of course he broke down, part by grisly part,
Assigned to a softer beat: features, art.

At an opening he met a poet
Who recommended verse instead of news.
Poetry was truth, she said, *points of view
Sharper than any photograph.* So he quit,
Penning villanelles by the ever-tolling
Campanile. Professors were extolling

The vaguer virtues—riffraff that they were—
Castrating words so that they lost focus
And definition. Soon the nebulous
Memories embedded in him would blur,
Even the girl with an arrow thrust into
Her heart, *Wamaka Og'naka Icante,*

Speaking of angels in her final breath—
Too sentimental, his mentors demurred.
He wrote about egrets, or rarer bird,
Using words like *shard, frond,* and *shibboleth.*
Critics with namby phobias assessed
His verse, revered it. And then he confessed.

Atheist Testimonies

I. *Prepositions*

Carl B. at Yale renounces faith in God
At nine-oh-eight a.m. His T.A. dyed
Her "do" an orange hue instead of auburn
As on the Clairol carton, and is gone
Punk against her will. Faith is brittle, friends;
Broken promises of beauty, splitting ends,

And inner office infatuations.
The T.A. never pinpoints his intentions,
So files no charge of gender harassment.
He weeps to see her tangerine-like tint
As pilgrims weep when Mary reappears
In Wal-Mart pumps. Something's insincere

About belief in *nether*world or *after*life—
Hereafter prepositions. Husband, wife
Take the other better, worse, for granted.
Take and leave their lovers, disenchanted.
There is no God or wingéd seraphim.
The girl's *beyond*, not over, under him.

II. *Premonitions*

Sue B. renounces faith in postal service
At twelve-fourteen p.m. She has a choice
To fix the plumbing rather than her teeth,
Or cap bicuspids. Let the cellar seep.
The children need new shoes or maybe soles.
They have been walking in, not *on*, puddles.

His check is late. Atheism has its perks,
A dim Darwinian logic that lurks
In elite habitats: *Man mounts T.A.*
To cinch survival of his DNA,
Relinquishing descendants to the state.
His singular role is to propagate

And publish his memoirs in *The Atlantic*.
Sue has lost her God, and now is frantic.
This afternoon her sons come home from school
To play their Segas in the basement pool
While mommy loiters at a campus tavern
And wonders when her ex will wander in.

III. *Propositions*

He wanders in—a mere coincidence.
An atheist obeys the laws of chance,
Rejects commandments like *Thou shalt not*
Covet nor commit adultery nor sit
Beside a Wiccan with Metallica hair.
The woman snubs him, swivels in her chair

And shields mascara eyes in mock salute
To some unseen power. Her pain's acute
And emanates from keen embarrassment.
If one must die, why not from harassment
In front of colleagues, students, strangers?
Why not release the canonized angers

In front of his spouse, whom she finally spies
In the corner booth? Sue is masking her eyes
In the same sad salute as the punk T.A.
Who started this, believing she was made
In the image of those Clairol models,
Their miraculous hair like an angel's.

Sans Nature

You wake to the usual sounds of flush toilet
Or pipe-gurgle, redolent steam of coffee-perk,
And mete your life by cups, quips Eliot,
Likely apostle. *What rocks or wastelands lurk?*
You drive to work and drive yourself to work
The slave hours of urban sprawl, brown-bag it,
The park too great a risk. So goes the week,
The seasons blend or cease. You inherit

The earth to whose core you must return,
Or in the crematory burn, your bones rent
Among the remaining lilies and legumes.
The worst part is that you know this. You earn
Every cardiac minute of your estrangement
Walking the malls and the indoor arboretums.

Hove

for Leon Daniel

You know me. And don't. You wouldn't recognize me
In the street, though I have stopped you there
Dead in your tracks. Outside a cafe maybe

In Des Moines—a greasy spoon, say—on a morning
Like any other. You put your two bits in the box,
Reached for a paper, and froze: our boys are napalming

Kids now instead of Vietcong. Can't place me?
From Adam? Try this: *In order to save the village,*
The colonel said, we had to destroy it.

It was said. I have the notes, after all
These years. And my rival Peter got it, too.
Word for word. The kind of quote you think

God made to stick in our skull. Did you hear that?
I asked Peter, knowing we did, knowing we would
Cable it from Saigon. The colonel was caught up

In the count—bodies laid out for us like mats—
But we were stunned. The war, for once, made sense:
To save Vietnam, we would have to destroy it.

That was long ago. I am where I like to be,
Near water, waiting for something to surface.
Atomic submarine, finally making a port call.

Years. Imagine living so long near sea-bottom?
Women on board, too! The stories that have to abound.
Husbands and wives all around me, happy as clams,

Waiting to become triangles. Toddlers about to meet
Dad for the first time. Know how you hate a neighbor?
Try living like a sardine with one for thirty months.

Enemies, getting a break. But today I think of myself.
I am getting a chance to write something joyful,
A phrase that has jangled in my mind since Jakarta,

Where I was when that tidal wave cleaned East Pakistan.
You don't remember it, but you should. Who cares about
Asia anyway? One hundred thousand people washed to sea,

A wave fifteen feet high that swept over miles of paddies
And took everyone who wasn't two flights up. Not many
Buildings that high in Bangladesh, the name now

For that place. Place of death. One hundred thousand
People—more than half of Des Moines, god damn it—
And you didn't give a diddly. Let bygones be.

They pay me to tell you, not to make you think.
Leave that for the poets! This is what I want to write,
To cap a story you would clip and save like a stamp:

And the ship hove into port. Sure, we're talking
Submarine. But you get one chance: *And the sub
Hove into port.* Not bad. The desk may let it by,

And out it would fly on tickertape of your hometown
Newspaper. Make the eggs go down easier at that
Greasy spoon. Why does it mean so much? Why

Would I even want to tell you? Maybe you think
I've a little romantic in me. War correspondent.
Trenchcoat, Casablanca. I'm a backwoods boy

Out of Tennessee, a box of a man with no neck
For a raincoat. Pop-bottle glasses that make
My eyes too big and blue for my ruddy skin

And cheeky face. But you would tell me
Your life story. Ask the colonel. Ask Peter,
The competition. We didn't cover the half of it.

When you cable for bets on the body count at Da Nang,
They bring you home. Things happen. Say a reporter
Like Kate gets lost in the tropical forest and collapses

In your arms twenty-five days after the funeral.
We thought she was dead. We gave her desk to a rookie
From New York. She stumbled into the bureau

Scraggly, mosquito-bit, barely able to punch
Her story. But we let her, waiting, waiting
For the last click of the keys, for the last

Syllable to clear the continent. Kate Webb.
You don't remember her, but I do. She had
A phrase and she got to use it: *It was like*

A butcher shop in Eden, beautiful but ghastly.
That should have gone over big in Des Moines.
That was romance. That was foreign corresponding.

This isn't. This is busy work before they ship me
To Tel Aviv or Beirut. But a nuclear sub is news
When you see it: beautiful, ghastly. Dock it

In Mobile, and Alabama becomes a dangerous place.
You wouldn't know it the way the women in front of me
Stare at the ocean, awaiting their beloved.

Yearningly. Now there's a word! Women have
Waited at ports for millennia. They have courage,
All right. But you can't pin it with a medal.

Once a woman showed me where her breast had been.
Can you imagine that? I was between tours
And making the rounds, handshaking with publishers

And doing a local exclusive for the greasy spoon.
It was news then. Betty Ford just went through it.
A mother in Virginia had the operation and wanted

To talk. I'm a man, after all. What do you say?
*Do you feel any pain? Do you cry in the night?
Does your husband love you the same way?*

I'll never forget. That wonderful, wise,
Elegant lady looked at me square and asked,
As if she knew me a lifetime—no, more than that—

A *millennium*, "Would you like to see?
Would you like me to take off my blouse?"
All I could do was nod. She unbuttoned it

Slowly, tenderly almost as a lover might
Share the intricate wounds of the heart.
"Now you know," she said. "You can write about it."

I am thinking of her now. Also of Kate.
I do whenever the story seems bigger than me.
And the sub hove into port. I feel good about it.

The desk will let it by. Here it comes, Kate,
I am getting the chance. People are cheering,
And a band behind me is playing the Navy song

About anchors and ships. But what comes is a black
Pod of a vessel making its way into easy waters.
"Hove" isn't right. A half-truth. A submarine "glides."

And the sub glided into port. Now that's bad.
The desk will ask what I am drinking.
What about you in Des Moines? Would you care

If a submarine "hove" a little on the front page?
I never lied before. Ask the colonel. Ask Kate.
Ask the woman who showed me where a breast had been.

Today the calm waters of Mobile, Alabama, are going to get
Rougher on the tickertape. I take it in, the slow dock
Of a submarine that can do more damage than a tidal wave,

The sailors and spouses eager again or wary,
An ensign refusing to smile for the cameras,
A toddler who struggles in the arms of a stranger.

I leave to make the call. Someone new is at the desk
In New York. Mike, out of college. He asks,
Who is this again? He doesn't know me from Adam.

But the voice is right, the way I dictate
Logo and dateline. He's ready now for the story.
Go ahead, he says. *And the sub hove into port.*

I continue from my notes, but he interrupts.
Flowery, he says. Can't use it. Just tell me
What it was like. *It was like a butcher shop*

In Eden, beautiful but ghastly. Pause.
He's got his hand over the phone and mumbles
Something. Something is mumbled back, and now

The editor is on the line. Hove, I tell him.
Not many people know it is the past tense of heave.
He wants to know, then, why we are using it.

I clear my throat. I want them to understand.
Every now and then, I say, there is a phrase
Somebody in Des Moines needs to hear. Today

It is, *And a sub hove into port.*
I wish it were a ship. I wish it had sails
That ruffled like a silk blouse, opening.

II
The Revisionist

The Revisionist:
On Original Sin

To have a woman who loved you once, who held you
In high regard as if you were a god
Mounted on bedrock in a temple,
The temple of beauty, or truth,
Who looked into your eyes as the gypsy looks
Into her glass and sees the future
Until your eyes become that future,
Blue or green or black or brown—
Fertile colors—water, seedling, mineral, soil,
As if she were planting time
Certain something would grow
She even revised the seasons,
Eliminated autumn and winter,
Lengthened summer and spring
So that life was blossom and bud, bud and blossom,

To have her who loved you once, hate you now,
To hold you in disregard,
To topple the temple god,
To look into your eyes as an archer looks
Into her scope at the spiral
Black hole and sees the past
Until your eyes become that past
Out of which nothing grew—
Sterile colors—beetle, weed, shale, dung;
She would gladly put them out, pluck them
With thumb and forefinger like onion bulbs
As if she were uprooting time,
Eliminating summer and spring,
Lengthening autumn and winter
So that life is dark and dormant, dormant and dark,

To have that woman who loved you hate you
Now is how Adam must have felt
When Eve told him to leave
The Garden after lying about the snake,
The seduction, the inevitable betrayal,
And when he would not,
How she stood there with Cain and Able at her side—
Part his/ part hers, *their* past/ *her* future—
And picked up the windfall apple,
The nearest weapon,
Taking a bite to the core as she wanted
To take a bite out of the core of his wormy heart,
And hurling it, then hurling another, and another,
Following him beyond the forbidden gates,
Until she, too, entered the world.

The Revisionist:
On Noah's Ark

You saw it coming, the flood of tears dammed finally
To a trickle. No one understands why you rented
The U-Haul and loaded it at 3 a.m. in the rain
While your husband was out of town again on business.

Lights flick on, off. Neighbors think you have gone
Crazy hitching the car and carrying the children
Bundled asleep in your arms, jiggled in their seats
For the journey. Time has come for hard decisions:

Dogs, cats, birds—yes, but tropical fish?
What about grease ants in your cabinets?
Mice under the bed, roaches in the sink?
Aren't they yours, too? Don't they set your hours—

Intimate beings—when you bake, love, shower?
Don't they serenade you, cantata of crickets
Or bebop of flies on the sill, squirrels on the roof,
Cicadas on the limbs of your favorite weeping willow?

How could you leave, how could you cope,
Without them? Everything here is doomed:
Heirlooms on the mantel, portraits on the wall,
The wicker rocker where you would wait for him,

Creaking like a craft off course. Like Noah
You know that people live or drown but take
Nature with them, even the fleas thumbing a ride.
The spiders will miss you, mosquitoes will mourn.

Who has loved you so well?

The Assassin Of Assisi

I threw the monkey wrench at Darwin
But he ducked
Under the bill of a platypus.
It struck Sir Isaac
Between the eyes at the cider tree,
And the whole world

Dimmed. When he came to,
He marveled at the alloy
And gave up alchemy,
Advancing the clock,
Discovering mechanics, laws of motion,
How bodies travel millennia in a line

Unless compelled
To act otherwise.
He cast the coordinates in the clay
At the base of the tree,
The wind kicking up,
Worms awriggle in the fallen cores,

The wrench on the horizontal plain
And his head on the vertical
Intersecting in a cross.
Thus, he was born again,
And I've been on the path ever since,
Posse of one

Atop an astral mule.
Assassin of science, I lost
My innocence at Assisi
Under the basilica. I know
Whose side, whose century
The cognoscenti honor in the annals,

But imagine the world
As it might have been
As the mule descended
Mount Subasio with its own laws
Of motion: simplicity, creation,
Love of all living things.

Coccinella 7–Punctata

Biologists say the creator
Had a fondness for beetles,
Queenly colors of a wingcase
More angelic than seraphim

Aflutter at the seat of all-
Being. Whoever made you
Kept re-making you until
You were divine as the seven

Dots on your back,
Red and yellow like apples
Out of Eden. Kill beetles,
And the hop fields burn:

Lady bug, lady bug,
Fly away home,
Your house is on fire,
Your children do roam. ...

Another judgment is upon us,
Our Lady. Blessed Coccinella,
Intercede as your namesake
Seldom does on our behalf.

SETI Sestina

NASA technicians send you best wishes:
Make us a megajoule particle beam.
We seek messiahs on microwave dishes.
How do you turn off a cancerous gene?
Replenish an ocean with edible fishes?
This is a beacon. Please intervene.

This is a beacon. Please intervene.
Biotechnicians may e-mail their wishes
To aliens on-line by particle beam,
Awaiting an answer on Microsoft dishes.
How do you turn off a cancerous gene
When people are eating mercurial fishes?

Our messiah forgives us and fishes.
This is a beacon. Please intervene.
Hubble technicians are transmitting wishes
To Point Omega whose particles beam
Cable on backyard microwave dishes.
"How do you turn off the video, Jean?"

"How do you turn off the video, Jean?"
She fries him a pan of mercurial fishes.
This is a beacon. Please intervene.
A biotechnician reports that he wishes
To bypass the megajoule particle beam
And cure a pandemic in petri dishes.

"Sears is having a sale on its dishes."
"Wal-Mart is discounting buttonfly jeans."
"Jimmy Hoffa swims with the fishes."
This is a beacon. Please intervene.
"Your personal psychic will satisfy wishes."
"Scotty is fixing the transporter beam."

Make us a megajoule particle beam
To see the messiah on microwave dishes,
Discover a cure for the cancerous gene,
Feed the plebeians by splitting two fishes.
This is a beacon. Please intervene.
Our technicians are patenting wishes,

Mutating fishes by particle beam,
While Jean in her kitchen washes the dishes
And SETI wishes that stars intervene.

Evangelists, Environmentalists

Evangelists like to flash backward
Playing records and tapes,
Listening for Lucifer in the low syllables.

Environmentalists like to flash forward
Tape-recording temperatures,
Looking for holes in the high altitudes.

Ev*angel*ists have halos; env*iron*mentalists,
Ores. Halogens. *Lists* of souls, species
Near extinction. Both believe in floods,

The mythology of lifeboats and whales.
One wants to save Jonah,
The other the orca whose song is a psalm.

Both damn man, prophesying doom
At the door. Donations are deductible.
One can't wait to get to heaven,

The other can't bear to leave earth.
One thinks that God will reward him.
The other thinks not.

The Entomologist

He knows now why insects will
Inherit the earth, your basic
Roach as prehistoric as a shark
Asphyxiating in an oil-slick,

Your basic ant colony
Overpopulated as any homosapien
City, with greater overall bio-
Mass. You have to admire them,

The compound eyes and antennae,
Exoskeletons of armor, stylets
Sharp as ice-pick, enough poison
In a scorpion to halt the heart.

So easy then to fall in love
With bugs as a boy, memorizing
Phyla while his parents fought
On a farm in Pennsylvania.

He would slip to the flowering
Meadow with a canning jar
Whose lid had no holes for air,
Mini coliseum, the specimens

He caught, the gladiators:
Lady-, water-, and lightningbugs,
Butter-, horse-, and dragonflies,
Roaches, hornets, honeybees—

Whatever a boy could trap.
He'd shake them up
And put the jar to his ear
As if holding a conch

To hear the ocean, marveling
At the hum of aerial insects
As they attacked the hand-
Held glass, not each other,

The crawlers on the bottom
Racing around the perimeter,
Playing dead. He did this
Countless times, and never

Did a slaughter ensue,
The captives too intent on
Overcoming a common plight,
Another reason to praise them

More than people. Put people
In an arena with lethal
Weapons and no hope of escape
And they butcher each other.

Insects at least had priorities.
So while his parents fought,
Their voices rising in crescendo,
Their marriage hopeless as a jar,

He became infatuated with
The esprit de corps of insects
Suffocating one by one,
In the air-tight death-chamber.

When he dumped out the remains,
He would hold them lovingly
In his palm, as if reading
The future, the importance

Of pinning the object
Of passion, classifying it,
Cataloguing its flaws,
Traits, and mating rituals

In clear focus now
Under the electron scope
Of his mind, remembering
How the roach would stir,

Drop from his palm,
And cast a sidelong glance
At him, knowing whose time
Was almost up, whose world.

Cicadas in New Jersey

They have migrated into the maples
Lining the boulevards, abandoning
The Meadowlands upon which stadiums

Have been built, complexes.
My sister complains
She cannot stand their singing,

Their ticks, buzzes, and groans
So familiar in the neighborhood
They drown out the fog horns of

Barge on the Passaic, rumble of
Rigs on the Turnpike, yammer of
Tires on the Parkway, clicks of

Trains on the trestles—
Not singing at all, she asserts,
A cacophony outside her window.

She cannot sleep with it open,
An inalienable right,
Her life ruled by racket.

In China cicadas sang princesses
To sleep in sanded cages of bamboo
Hung by moonlight in the summer.

But in Lyndhurst, my sister grows
Insomniac. She wants them dead,
Mort. This is so unlike her,

Gentle creature. I have seen her
Sweep spiders and beetles
On front pages of The Star-Ledger,

Apt obit, rather than exterminate.
I have witnessed her scrubbing
Chicken in baptismals of Tupperware

Rather than risk salmonella,
But now she wants to climb
A maple and aerosol the ozone

Out of cicadas. She has called me,
A killer like Sun Tzu, to learn
The art of war, and I tell her:

Know the enemy, the ocelli eyes,
The timbals at the base of
The abdomen that make the music.

Know the terrain, the disappearing
Wetlands, the endangered trees,
The mounds of refuse on the horizon.

Know the weather, how the cicada
Predicts patterns, quakes, warmings,
Why, the ones outside her window

Burrowing there in 1983,
Ready at last to rise and copulate,
Their own Y2K problem. So beware,

I warn, we may all come back
As cicada in the next millennium
When spider, beetle and ubiquitous

Roach, rule, when cities will be
Silent even in New Jersey.
She thanks me—*So long, brother*

Since I have told her a story—
How time flies, things change;
But thinks that she can sleep now,

Listening to the serenade.

Spoon River Garland

New deaths in the cemetery of
Edgar Lee Masters' *Anthology*

1. AIDS

Daily I search the realms of Hades—
                    "The Unknown"

You know the cause of death but not my name
Quilted like initials on a sleeve in
Scarlet, the blood color. I shared the same
Needle as my idol Hester Prynne

And sewed my fate. I overheard your whispers,
Overlooked your sleights. You broke my will,
Then buried me without one, as a pauper;
You marked me every day when I was ill,

Then lowered me into an unmarked plot
As if to quarantine me here for good.
Now the roles are reversed. Now I can out
You from the grave in gratitude and would

Engrave your future, suture it on gowns,
Knowing whose time is up and whose is down.

2. DOMESTIC VIOLENCE

There is no marriage in heaven,
But there is love—"Sarah Brown"

Possession is the law on earth, 9/10ths.
I died for love or lack of, take your pick.
You stalked me daily in the labyrinth
Of neighborhoods, a deadly hide-and-seek,

Then beat our kids and sued for custody.
Possession is the law in limbo, too,
1/10th. You walk there like an amputee
Searching for the arm you used or drew

Against your family. *Guess who owns it?*
Possession is the law in hell: your soul
Belongs to you alone. No one wants its
Fractions and fractures. But here I am whole,

You can't control me anymore—devoid,
Dispossessed—so that I can be, by God.

3. CANCER

> *To pervert the truth, to ride it for a purpose—*
> "Editor Whedon"

Sometimes a word infects and then inflames
Communities. We want our records purged,
Our sins erased. Accomplishments proclaimed.
Reporters euphemize when others judge,

Noting this "lengthy illness" and that "un-
Timely death" or "sudden one." Mine was long
In the making. The organs, one by one,
Began to purge themselves: tongue, liver, lung.

Disease may be indelible as ink,
But so is the truth. I smoked and blew smoke
Where the publisher pointed. Then I drank
To forget what or whom the headlines broke.

No headline breaks for me, my ashes blown,
Down the polluted streams and out of town.

4. ACADEMIC SUICIDE

> *Here is a joke of cosmic size—*
>   "Professor Newcomer"

Which is dumber: the reasons people kill
Themselves or the techniques? The rhetoric
Of martyrdom or the arithmetic of pills?
You build your mausoleums brick by brick

Then leave word on an answering machine
Or under refrigerator magnets.
You diagnose yourself in magazines
Or in discussion groups on Internet,

Analyzing tenure and denial,
The urge to off the dean as effigy.
They found my note in the permanent file,
As eloquent as any elegy,

And me after hours in the office,
Perrier and Prozac, the cocktail of choice.

5. DOUBLE SHOOTING

> *I was sick, but more than that, I was mad—*
> "Rosie Roberts"

I would have quizzed my executioner
With a curtsey: *Was it good for you, too?*
I used to launder my husband's collars
Bespattered with mascara residue.

If anger is a stage, then so is this
Eerie inability to express
Ire under psychoanalysis
Or suspicion. At last you end the stress

In a parked pickup with a shotgun rack
While your spouse urinates on a culvert.
He kept on belittling me, his back
Beckoning me like a cotton target.

I fired. When he fell, I felt his pain
And then the guilt, so I fired again.

6. ADDICTION

She cried, and kissed me, and said it was cruel—
                              "Roscoe Purkapile"

I had one wife and one dependency.
If I could, I'd have had several
Spouses and no addictions or many
Addictions, no wives. Mine was a lethal

Mix of marital and criminal acts.
She would not listen to soliloquies;
She heard them all before. Instead she packed
Clean clothes in the valise and gave me keys

To the good car, happy I was taking
Addiction with me like a hitchhiker
On a trip. I knew the point she was making
About sex drive but drove to street walkers

And let addiction out so I could come
Back to her. One day it followed me home.

7. HOMELESSNESS

> *[T]he conservatives were never sure of me—*
> "George Trimble"

As indicators go, so go the people:
Economies are doppler, overcast.
You don't wake up in the street. You trickle
There with a theory or pool with a forecast

Until the tax and census takers miss
You in the count. You're invisible now
Following the Atlas to abyss:
Living in your car, slogging through the snow,

Wearing entire wardrobes on your back.
What do you make of a society
That tallies housing starts but loses track
Of homeless? They have no identity

In subways or doorways, under debris.
I ceased to be before I ceased to be.

8. ANGEL DUST

> *You did not seem to be afraid of the flesh—*
> "Father Malloy"

I met monsignor in the vestibule,
Robed and disrobed him in the sanctuary.
But there was none for me, bullied at school,
Abused and beaten at home. He took me

Inbetween confessions (sometimes during)
And as penance coerced apologies.
Then gave me communion and a warning:
Tell your blessings, not your rosaries.

I served as altar boy, alter ego,
And soon feared the priesthood more than God's wrath.
So I left him and the church. Years ago
I stopped fearing and believing in both,

Overdosing on dust—hopeless, unwhole—
Letting them divvy the body and soul.

9. BYSTANDER

Who snapped the toy pistol against my hand?
                    "Charlie French"

I was watching a local gangsta go
Down in the parking lot of the project,
Cops on top of him like a rodeo
Steer on ESPN, roping a suspect,

When some clown behind me snaps a Mattel
Automatic in my palm, a perfect fit,
Cap gun with a magazine clip rattle-
Tat-tatting pretend bullets, and lickety-split

Before I even realize, I'm dead—
Rattle-tat-tatting in a tunnel toward Jesus—
Still toting the cap gun like an airhead
Aiming at the Lord, compliments Toys-R-Us,

Another stick-up in paradise, pardner:
So he puts up his arms and surrenders.

10. CHILD ABUSE

*I was among multitudes of children
Dancing at the foot of the mountain—*
            "Elijah Browning"

You end up in a place without parents
But sense somebody gazing down on you
In the pine-shadows where the moonlight went
Laser on your shoulders, healing the bruise.

You end up in a place without arguments
But sense somebody watching out for you
In the creek-shallows where the twilight sent
Ripples on broken legs, so that they grew.

You can climb those pines now without slipping
On limbs and hang there, as the others do.
You can cross those shallows without tripping
On rocks and end up any place you choose,

Even home again with your parents who
Do not argue or lay a hand on you.

11. ANOREXIA

My wife lost her health,
And dwindled until she weighed scarce ninety pounds—
                                                    "Willard Fluke"

My husband looked at other women and I,
In the mirror. I wanted what he saw
In magazines and the models of high
Fashion. At first I covered up my flaws

With a new wardrobe, looser knits and slacks.
He said he liked them tight. I exercised
Other options—all manner of Nordic Tracks—
And cut out sweets, went down another size.

I lost fat to gain affection. So shed
Pound upon pound till he summoned a priest,
Accepting wine and water but no bread.
I hungered for a different host, decreased

My in-take again, thinking I had better
Please him and stop breathing altogether.

12. DRIVE-BY

> *And there would be your world of guns!—*
> "Ippolit Konovaloff"

In this city everyone wants a piece
Of the action, a little turf to protect.
You can set up shop without police
Loitering on the corner and collect

What is coming to you. Maybe you spy
A car in an alley or parking lot
With arsenals inside. In this city drive-bys
Are commoner than taxis. You get shot

Leaning against a lamppost in the a.m.
When a vehicle revs in the avenue,
Windows down and bullets bright. Taking aim
You raze the light before they raise you

In an open hearse and close the casket,
Making or settling a score. You forget.

13. CARJACKING

> *All I could say was "Don't, Don't, Don'"*
> *As he aimed and fired at my heart—*
>   *"Tom Merritt"*

It's Americana with anti-lock brakes
And dual airbags, a better technology
Than horses but bearing their names: Broncos,
Mustangs, Colts. It's part of our history,

Americana with nine-millimeters
And talon bullets, a better weapon
Than the Smith & Wessons or Derringers
That won the West. There were highwaymen

Who murdered you with a Colt for a colt
Long before interstates in this country
Or carjackers. Slain in an assault
I was abandoned on US 80

In a panorama of memory,
Reliving the American story.

14. BOMBING

> *Only the chemist can tell, and not always*
> *the chemist, what will result—*
>   "Trainor, The Druggist"

You time a bomb the way you do a car:
In the garage, tinkering with cylinders.
According to neighbors, you're a regular
Guy with a gripe against the Post Master

Or mass transit. You may rely on it,
Always the delivery to consider.
You time a bomb the way you do a sonnet:
In feet. You want to flee the disaster

In tact, trigger it by remote control,
And watch it at home on local stations.
Make a statement or demand. That's the goal.
But I was more con man than technician,

Timing my bomb to boost an alibi,
The shards of my life like a prophecy.

15. THE GARLAND

You know the cause of death but not our names.
We died for love or lack of, take your pick:
Our sin's erased. Accomplishments proclaimed,
We built our mausoleums brick by brick.

If anger is a stage, then so is this.
You will not listen to soliloquies
Following the Atlas to abyss:
Tell your blessings, not your rosaries.

Before you even realize, you're dead
On limbs and hang there as the others do,
Accepting wine and water but no bread.
You raise the Light before It raises you

In a panorama of memory,
The shards of your life like a prophecy.

Plath at Primrose Hill

*Upon renting a London flat occupied once by Yeats,
Plath reportedly opened to a line from one of his plays,
which read, in part: "I will get the house ready."*

You wander home to William, Fitzroy Road,
As if to hush the filibuster muses
One, Two, Three. Your days are numbered like an ode

Anointing laureates in each abode.
When letters stop, the poems come in deuces.
You wander home to William, Fitzroy Road,

But soon become the swan that Leda rode.
Your hero mesmerizes, then seduces:
One, two, three. ... You like to number "day" and "ode"

Recorded in a diary whose code
The coroner deciphers as he chooses.
You wander home to William, Fitzroy Road,

Escaping yet another episode
With husband back in Devon. He recluses.
"I. II. III." Your numbered days are like an ode

With strophe, antistrophe, and epode.
How easily a tragedy reduces!
You wander home to William, Fitzroy Road
123. Your days are numbered like an ode.

Death Of A War Hero

for Emmanuel Apap (1919-94)

So many Rambo movies have been made
It's hard to consider a war hero
Being anything other than Anglo
Or dumb as Forrest Gump playing ping-pong
In the MIA alleys of Haiphong.

My immigrant uncle was brown and meek.
When he cried, rivulets would map his cheek
Like swollen tributaries of the Rhine.
Someone issued him an M1 carbine
And he used it. He resembled a rookie

Sensation for the legendary Yankees—
Yogi Berra—which was something back then.
He lived in the shadow of that icon,
Squat as a catcher with a different mask:
Death. The grim reaper is not as grotesque

As you think. Say "Emmanuel" to it.
Once he entrapped an entire unit
In the bloody Ardennes and ambushed them
With other assassins. The stratagem
Worked. By nightfall, the Nazi field marshal

Had lost a dozen men and his morale,
Lower than the Feuhrer in his bunker.
The Wehrmacht was routed. He could suffer
This tiny defeat, hoisting a hankie
And waving the way fans do at Yankee

Stadium when a rookie points his bat.
Emmanuel pointed a bayonet
At the enemy and told them to drop
Their rifles in a pile. The sniping stopped.
The Americans emerged from the woods.

Again my uncle had beaten the odds
And encircled a field marshal with a *von*
Inbetween his names, a blueblood Saxon
Analyzing another rabble of "Yanks"
And bearing a sidearm with ruby and onyx

Swastikas on the handle. My uncle stepped
Forward with those sorry cheeks. He had wept
Because he slew Aryan boys littler
Than he who were wearing the same Hitler
Insignia on infantry uniforms

Instead of pinstripes. He noted the sidearm.
The field marshal noted the rifle-pile,
Wanting to fight again. He could reconcile
His capture, it seemed, but not his captor,
Daring Emmanuel to massacre

Prisoners or permit them to retake
Positions. The German made a mistake,
As if this was the end of an inning,
Not a battle, with my uncle brandishing
A bat and not a bayonet. He looked up.

He was always looking up in the hope
Those looking down would see beyond the mask.
"What gives you the right?" the German asked
In the flawless American lingo
Nazis learned along with "DiMaggio"

And "Berra." My uncle hated baseball.
He aimed and unloaded a bullet-hail,
Winging the officer's bluebloody head.
"*This* gives me the right," Emmanuel said
In a language everyone understood.

Later that year outside Weimar he would
Help free Buchenwald. The inmates amassed
Along the barb wire fence as he passed
To open the gate. They stood eye-level
And saw death incarnate. They knew it well,

And the name "Emmanuel" meant nothing.
Substitute father, he meant everything
To me growing up in the stadium-shadow.
Yogi Berra was back, hawking "Yoo-hoo"
In a bowling alley off US 3.

My uncle suffered a half century
What we call Post Traumatic Stress Syndrome.
The holocaust was real in our home.
"Each life you took," I told him, "you gave back
Liberating that camp." He wouldn't talk.

Words were meaningless. But they could still haunt.
Emmanuel died at a restaurant
Without help of the Heimlich maneuver,
Something the enemy pulls in a war.
Finally the paramedics arrived

Encircling him, managing to revive
A heart beat by jump-starting the body
As mechanics do a car battery,
Attaching the electrical cables.
Emmanuel had left the vehicle

Of life idling there by accident,
Tethered to tubes in a hospital tent.
Soon his fingers curled as if in anger
Trying to grasp invisible triggers
In that room. Doctors cut intravenous

And no one in the name of Christ Jesus
Picketed that decision. He was just
Another survivor going to waste
Without food and water, the iron gate
Opening wide so that he could escape.

III
The Visionary

Consciousness

When, precisely, did I fathom the sublime
Acid ironies of being: *I am
What I was and will be*, a jumble of genes,
My 4% brain flicked on like DNA,
The time to change already having ended

In adolescence? In 1960
Swaying in left field to tinny rock'n'roll,
I made first contact as my friend O'Hara
Made first base, the ball rolling to a stop
At the tip of a high-top Ked. I dropped

The transistor radio and looked up
At the sky—why up always at the sky?—
And knew that fate was fixed, a target
Like O'Hara rounding second base;
Yet felt electric, almost Whitmanesque,

And rocketed that ball to beat the runner
Heading home, where I would hasten later,
Asking my Mother why the life before me
Wobbled like a loose erector set
With screws that only tighten clockwise,

The thudding orb already in the mink-
Oiled middle of Mustardo's mitt,
Falling to the plate where O'Hara slid
Safe as usual, nine years from Vietnam.
Mustardo wept, eleven years from Yale,

And light years from awareness, I yelled *Yes!*

Life's Ineffable Edge

What came came at top speed into the dunce
Skull cap of fontanel, and suddenly
I understood the universe in pieces
As if the cerebellum had a circuit
Hot-wiring my neurons. My new son
Whinnied when it happened and awoke
From half-sleep paradise of mother-suckle.

But this was not the fabled light of Christ
That comforts even at misfortune's edge.
For I had toed that precipice before
Beside two daughters lost in white-out
Pediatric wards. I could confront
The doppelganger light and still endure.
My son and wife beheld me eerily,

Silently, the way that pilgrims might,
Not at the phosphor-flick of seraphim
Nor at diffuse enlightenment of Zen
Nor at the near-death aftershock of being.
This light became a binary flash
Of terrifying cosines I could trace
With magic fingertips on moonlit walls,

Reciting quantum physics and equations
Easily as lullabies, emerging odds
Of origins on prebiotic Earth
Among a hundred billion bluer planets.
I know we're not alone and yet divine
A purpose in each quark and quandary,
Humbled by my nanosecond knowledge.

Why me? I ask my wife who buried babies
And nearing forty bore another one.
Why not the angel-aura of my daughters
Aflutter in the tunnels of transcendence?
My son is cooing, suckling her again.
"Because you're trusting nature," she replies,
"And nature knows that you can take it now."

—for Diane

First Love Poem To My Son

No one has to tell me the importance
Of fatherhood, pain of that first hard pitch
In the abdomen. Your mother took her stitch
In time. We watched you dance your baby dance
On pillowed breasts and nothing since makes sense
About this Spartan love which enriches
As it separates on the bed, your niche
Between us. Position's all in romance

But this ardor is beyond me, someplace
Deep-seated, like a door in adolescence:
You civilize me, son, when you embrace
My finger in your whole palm. That's power,
Joy. The angelic force of innocence
Clinging as I hoist you and you hover.

Two Sounds

for my son

Grandmother came here in the cargo hold
Of a great vessel and loved the tap of rain
On roofs, the ocean ever in her ears,
Grooved cornucopias that echo still
In this empty shell like a wavelength.
Can you hear the soothing rattle-tap-tap
Gutter-drip, her fingertip on your pane?
You, too, will lose and find me in this hymn

At 40, dreading another dawn. Listen
Then to the arias of robin and starling
Grandmother fed with bread I did not eat
On her lawn, happy to wake to the warbling,
As we wait now, sleepless but together.
  I have loaned you these legacies of sound
To outlast the apparitions of light
Which always fade, as I will, in the night.

Your Mother's Harmonica

An anthem is only as tin as your ear.
You think you know your mother, surely
That, the umbilical rhythms. You hear
Her concertina rib cage, chimpanzee,

Bellowing "My Country 'Tis of Thee"
In immigrant tenement flats
And come out singing. Even timpani
Kettles in the kitchen where you sat

Rattled, a curious accompaniment,
Footfalls pocking the linoleum
Hardwax with choreographed dents,
An elaborate code you could palm

And call home. Now you honor her
Transposing the mysterious word
Embossed on her handmade Hohner—
Wandervoegel—"migrating bird"?

Your mother flew under a Union Jack,
The usual exodus, and would tap
"God Save The Queen" as practical joke
On constables dubbing her wop

In imperial ports of call.
They stamped her visa and valise
As she whirled in the holding cell,
Wheezing in musical Maltese

Sweet land of liberty. She conned them
With a skeleton key of C
And cut time of a national anthem.
This country 'tis of thee, chimpanzee,

And not your poetry, God forbid,
Opening doors in America
The same way your mother did
On Ellis Island with a harmonica,

Cradling it in her palms and placing
Her mouth on lips of the mouth organ—
Blowing and sucking, blowing and sucking—
The song you learned when you were born.

—for Joey Attard

My Brave Asthmatic
for my daughter

Asthma has no solstice but a season:
Her last breath is her last breath. She earns it
As the miler earns the tape: chest forward,
Panting. She knows the atmosphere is spored
By autumn foliage, but a neighbor burns it,
And embers descend on her like demon.

Then winter arrives with its chill reason.
Her last snow is her last snow. She can sense
An avalanche of the alveoli
Welling in her like slush. While others ski
The mountain slope or slalom, she laments
Her lot. Spring is yet another treason,

A conspiracy of honeybees on
Hibiscus. *Her last rose is her last rose.*
She may lose innumerable lovers
Refusing their perfume or sprays of flowers.
She may wheel out of proms in orchid clothes
Into hospital emergencies on

Gurneys, already gowned for the occasion.
Last summer is her last summer. Knowing,
She hoards an arsenal of aerosol
And aims her inhaler like a pistol,
Holed up indoors to endure the mowing,
The myriad repellents. Eyes wizen.

Even influenza has a season:
Her last virus is not her last virus.
It navigates the labyrinth of vein,
Embeds within her shrunken lungs again,
Suppressing pleas and the esophagus,
And yet my brave asthmatic wheezes on.

Showing the House

Our daughter's boyfriend chipped his collarbone
Assaulting her on prom night in the doorwell.
He stumbled on the cedar trim and fell
Across these tiles, cracking that corner one.

Of course, we will replace it. To the left
Where empty stockings hang upon the hearth,
I've nicked the drywall, measuring the height
Of growing children. One stops at two feet

Because of meningitis. We'll patch the hole
Best we can. Accompany me to the kitchen.
I made the oak cupboards with porcelain
Handles, impressing my wife in the trial

Separation. She overlooked the flaws—
Loosening dovetails, unlatchable doors—
Quite fixable. I knelt on no-wax floors
By the double sink. Perhaps we should pause

At the bay window to gaze at the in-ground
Pool by the unweeded wisteria
In the garden. The dog's buried near there.
Nothing we can do about that. She drowned

In a thunderstorm, and we'll mend the liner.
In this bedroom we conceived our only son
On a chilly night. We thought we were done
Rearing children and cuddled each other

Because I never caulked that drafty pane.
But will tend to it before closing.
So let us know whether there is anything
We can do by way of repairs before then.

This old house is happier than it seems.
You may think of us within these lacquered walls
Late at night and hear the familial calls,
Assuming our debts, resuming our dreams.

The Conifer King

At the closing, he cut the final check
To live what days were left inside a dream
Estate with covered deck on cul-de-sac.
No one ciphered the unfathomable sum
Of agoraphobia in a suburb:
He had a lot but not land. He would hear
The van mufflers of mothers at the curb
Instead of finches, mourning dove and deer,
Inhaling fumes of garbage truck and bus
Instead of conifer and eucalyptus.

He also had a pie-shaped plat of lawn
To mow in tidy rows and manicure,
Uprooting dandelions in the dawn
Mist of neighborly repellant. They'd manure.
They'd sprinkle during drought clandestinely
And wheeze their asthma manifesto
From open window, bedroom balcony,
Admiring the astroturf below.
One day he had enough and dug a line
In which to plant a moat of spruce and pine

Around his property, walling neighbors out.
They watched him mulch the trees as evergreen
As Gawain's knight and near as animate
In the encroaching shade. They had foreseen
The loosed needles and unlucky clover,
The dandelion crop and clumps of flax
On an unmown yard of pointillist color.
The gathered mob gawked. But they did not ax
The teal windbreak of the conifer king
Or complain, spraying twice as much in spring

So the acid rain filled his moat-like swale.
Root-balls rotted and soon the needles browned.
Grass grew green again and the suburb, hale.
No one said a word about what happened,
Awaiting trucks to haul the trunks away.
Finches roosted for a while inside the firs,
Brittle cages. The dove and deer would stray
To nearby fields of subdevelopers
Annexing farms and leveling wetland,
Native wood. The conifer king let stand

The dead symbolic trees, what could have been,
Had he eluded status and later, wealth.
Now he knew the seasonal routine
Like yard- and clockwork, tending lawn and health.
Observing holidays. He hung plastic eggs
At Easter on his trees, replacing cones;
At Christmastide, blue lights around the twigs
As if to revive them; and candy canes.
The mob gawked. Children caroled and cajoled
Parents to plant conifers, till his estate sold.

—for Russ Baird

Forty in Southeast Ohio

I plant conifers and buy a timber
Wolf from a poacher in Vinton County.
He sells venison all season and keeps
Uncertified kennels, pups with papers:
Recycled *Athens News*. "It's a husky,"
He tells me. An eager ex-NewYorker

I still think honesty speaks with a twang.
Fact is, I want a wolf and a forest
The way that men in my city want rings
And gold chain. The only rings here are trunks
Unveiling ax and age, the gilt twilight
Scissoring the limbwork of pine and spruce

On moonslopes of Appalachian hollows.
Before the mines and Millfield disaster,
Wolves roved the Mohawk hillsides unhindered
As my own silvery she-bitch. She bounds
The fallen birch like nimble doe and howls
Among the hemlocks, their feathery tops

Asway in memory's forgotten breeze.
At forty in southeast Ohio, you learn
Life drops its cone with a seed deep inside
And needs a brush-fire to free. I dig
Another sapling row and she, a mole,
Shaking her bandit muzzle—no, no, no—

Till blood drains out of that buried creature
Too low on the totem pole of food chain.
I shake my head with her and whisper *No!*
To the poacher stalking me all season
In mid-life brushes with fate and ignite
My seed-fire now, howling to these slopes.

—for Lady Borton

Wolf

I have a dog, don't have a dog
Apace in a runnel of moon-glow.
She whittles fang on patio
And builds a den out of split log.

What I do have howls in the fog
Boondock of white-pine Ohio
With bobbing tail like silver doe.
In November dawn, hunters jog

Toward and away from my dog
Parting the goldenrod meadow
Like red sea. She races by cow
Pond and pie, pup tent and bog

Right at them. What I have won't wag
Or bark or fetch ball when I throw.
She stalks me like a caribou
When I turn my back on her and shrug.

I have a dog, don't have a dog
Tunneling under the fencerow
And over the pawprinted snow,
Undoing her collar and tag.

What I do have hops on groundhog
Ascending to see its shadow
Or growls underground in the burrow,
Boring her snout. She nips my leg

Because I am her underdog,
A beta wolf incognito
In wool clothing who doesn't know
How to moon-bay, nuzzle or dig:

But she teaches me not to beg
To the zookeep of Zen or crow
And to worship the here and now
Like a dog would, if she is a dog.

—for Skyah

The Boy Who Would Be Pope

His mom, who loves another lesbian,
Sighs in my kitchen. Her hair has gone gray
Living too long in the Appalachian

Hillside of Ohio, where local girls pray
To the patron saint of periods, or drop
Out of school. Her son is ten and can play

Rockabilly on my Kimball, hip hop
By heart. His mother is humming off key,
Half-listening as she clears the tabletop

And thinks. The lover's on the balcony.
Someone said an unkind word, or a few,
So they are missing the son's jamboree

In the next room. I drift to him on cue,
Hoping the women talk it out, or cope.
The music stops. "What do you want to do,"

I ask him, awkwardly, "when you grow up?"
I think he will say *play the piano*
Or *baseball*. But he confesses, "Be Pope."

The women eavesdrop in the hallway now.
"This way," he explains, "I can change the rule
And moms can marry moms." He would allow

Men to wed men, too, without ridicule,
And holds out both palms like His Eminence
Bestowing blessings or forgiveness. "Cool,"

He says, jazzing a hymn so they can dance.

—for Linn and Pattie

The Wedding Tree

A gift as all trees are, her Hoopsii,
A hybrid bluer than the borrowed sky
Of Colorado. She planted the spruce
For good luck, the cones as hard as promise,

And had her husband stake it like a heart,
Pounding rods of nitrogen in the dirt.
That first year she composted what she cooked,
Leftover eggs easy, the artichoke

Salads with bean sprouts, the greens he refused,
Though she always boiled for two. If he fussed
She would scrape his plate on the Hoopsii's
Warm and crackling mulch. Sometimes she would cry

On the wedding tree, as if to soak it,
Emptying a perforated bucket.
No one could explain why the Hoopsii
Stunted when he left her but did not die,

Another dim pathetic fallacy.
When they divorced, dividing property,
She potted the evergreen in a bowl
And set it on a city window sill

Where the needles blued diminutively
As on an Asian ornamental tree
Handed down through fallow generations.
Her conifer lives on that sill like patience,

A reminder. She forgave her first spouse
And wed a younger one who loves her spruce,
As small as hope and sorry as romance,
But blue all the same, in sheer defiance.

The Gift of Cash

to Diane, on our anniversary

It has come to this, the year of currency
Before the silver, gold. I ought to roam
Perfumed boutiques, their silken finery
Puddling through my fingers, or hurry home
With maudlin Hallmark in my hand. "Honey,"
It would read, "no bard can pen the poem
To celebrate our love." *Try*, you would say.

I am trying. These crisp Jacksonian bills
Symbolize my half-done life. Ambition kills
A man or he kills it to put away
The tidy sum. My sum is *you*. So pay
The piper tapping at the windowsills.
Our love endures without the ribbon-frills
Because we own it, if nothing else today.

Markers

Whenever we pass by the stone cape cod
We believed once we would own with pine trees
On both sides of the pebble drive downhill
To the blacktop, we slow the van and tell
The otherwise tedious liturgies
Of wedlock. But listen longingly and nod

Evenings on the river esplanade, walk
Among perennials—the candytuft
Or omnipresent ivy on the levees—
Reporting the return of migrant geese.
We digress and drift with cottonwood fluff,
Having heard it all before. Yet still talk

About daylilies, the orange ones
Repotted at the cedar bungalow
Long ago, where our only son was born;
Then we invoke genetic markers, mourn
The RH antigens of embryo,
And so employ the same old lexicons,

Reciting wounds and wonders of our lives
Like rosaries. Markers save a marriage,
For we measure ourselves and change by them,
And all is well, or well as it may seem
At millennium's end in middle age,
Knowing what comes comes again, then leaves.

Distortions

> *Wendy Freedman has been on the trail of this mystery for a decade. . . . To the distress of many, [she's] found the cosmos could be younger than many stars are thought to be*—Time, 6 March 1995

> The stars are only a backdrop for
> The human condition—Robert Penn Warren

Even the anti-transcendentalist
Robert Penn Warren believed in No Time
On whose edge he is sitting T-shirtless,
Grinning at the Hubble lens. Suddenly

The universe is younger than the stars
Clustering around him. Give a woman
Her own satellite, and the right software,
And she cubes the constellations a la

Picasso, parsecs of a deity
Whose mass has gone critical in NASA
Equations, those cosmic wrinkles in time.
At light speed even Robert Penn Warren

Waxes nostalgic for the *ubi sunt*
Days of hard science. A real man relied
On Polaris instead of orbiting
Polaroids to navigate home. Back then

Everything seemed linear, determined:
You began and ended and couldn't be
Older than your mother or two places
On the continuum at the same time.

—for Carol Muske

Quantum Bluebird

The physicist bird-watches
Not for the aesthetics
But as thought-experiment
In a field where a fox,
Unseen, starves in the chickweed.
The physicist has moved
Electrons with his mind,
Propelling them as wave
Or particle. Maybe
Electrons move *his* mind.
In any case, acts of
Observation occur
Now. The quantum bluebird
Appears atop a cone
Atop a spruce. He believes
The bird will fly away;
No—*The bird flies away*,
He thinks, because it is
Quantum, because electrons
Have flown upon command.
Or maybe electrons
Anticipate his thoughts
As readers do endings,
Trolling a syllable
Ahead of the creator.
The quantum bird is still
A particle atop
A cone atop a spruce
In a field where a fox
Paces in the chickweed.

The physicist believes
The bird will stay awhile;
No—*Stay awhile,* he thinks.
But now the bluebird flies
Because it senses fox.
The physicist has failed
His thought-experiment,
Though quantum bird and he
Will fluctuate between
Particle stream and wave
In REM-dreams yet to come.

   —for Drs. Wagner and Findlay

Assemblies of God

To be made in the image of deus
And deny it—your body, a masquerade—
To tally the beads of your abacus
And ascertain losses, the burial spade

In the dug meadow. This is an aubade
To mourners awaiting the miraculous
At parlor or pew. As virgins prayed
To be the maiden image of deus

Vaulting over a divine precipice,
You pray too. Everyone seems on crusade
Inviting cybersex or succubus.
Deny it, and your body masquerades

As mortuary wallflower, arrayed
For the planting. You make an exodus
Wailing, and no seas part as you are laid
To tally the beads of your abacus

Or the ebony sheep in the stratus,
Thank lucky clusters in the Pleiades:
Ashes to ashes, stardust to stardust.
And loss is certain as the burial spade.

You went nova before novena, rayed
Gamma before Alpha and Omega. Thus,
Life is not illusion, nor death charade,
But light, you are light yet and synthesis
To be made.

Millennium's End

Where are the Mahicans whose name means "wolf"
In the wolf-less mountains of the Catskill?
The Tasmanians whose rocks are relics
In the marsupial uplands of evolution?
The Congoids of the tropical basin?
The Caribs who met Columbus, the Celts
Who met the Norse in their holocaust sloops?

We, too, are explorers but cannot find them
In our modems and books. We know all about
Eur -asians and -arabs, the yearlings of war.
Show us the lost tribes of Israel and Germania
So we may follow the roads to Rome, annul
The laws of endangerment, and love each other
When love goes the way of the last Aleut.

Acknowledgments

Poems in this collection originally appeared in the following magazines:

Chariton Review—"Confessional Poetry" and "Millennium's End" under the title "Genera Ubi Sunt"
Clockwatch Review—"The Assassin of Assisi" and "Cicadas in New Jersey"
The Formalist—"Plath at Primrose Hill" and "Showing the House"
Georgia Review—"Your Mother's Harmonica" and "The Revisionist: On Noah's Ark"
Harper's—"The Revisionist: On Noah's Ark" (reprint)
Italian Americana—"The Gift of Cash"
Kansas Quarterly—"Articles of Insurrection"
Michigan Quarterly Review—"Shooter Rules"
Nimrod—"Hove"
Poet and Critic—"Evangelists, Environmentalists" and "Coccinella 7-Punctata"
Poet's Voice (Austria)—"The Revisionist: On Original Sin"
Prairie Schooner—"Assemblies of God" and "Spoon River Garland"
Quarterly West—"Distortions" and "Sans Nature"
Shenandoah—"The End of Civility"
Spoon River Poetry Review—"First Person" under the title "The Body Genetic"
Tar River Poetry—"SETI Sestina"
Texas Review—"First Love Poem to my Son"
TriQuarterly—"The Entomologist"
Web del Sol—"Atheist Testimonies" and "The End of Zeal"

"Hove" also appears in *For a Living: The Poetry of Work* (Univ. of Illinois Press, 1994)
"Bones" appears in the anthology *Life on the Line* (Negative Capability Press, 1993)
"Plath at Primrose Hill" was reprinted in *Anthology of Magazine Verse and Yearbook of American Poetry*
"Spoon River Garland" won an Ohio Arts Council Award
"Conifer King" also appears in Urban Nature (Milkweed Editions, 2000)
"Death of a War Hero" and "Two Sounds" appear in the anthology *American Diaspora: Poetry of Exile* (University of Iowa Press)

About the Author

Michael J. Bugeja is author of 16 books of nonfiction, fiction, and poetry. His poetry collections include *Talk*, University of Arkansas Press (1997); *Flight from Valhalla*, Livingston University Press (nominated for a Pulitzer Prize); *Platonic Love* and *After Oz*, both from Orchises Press; *What We Do For Music*, Amelia Press; *The Visionary* from Taxus Press in Exeter, England, (American reprint/Orchises Press). His creative writing awards include a National Endowment for the Arts fellowship, fiction, and an Ohio Arts Council fellowship, poetry. He is on the Advisory Board of *Writer's Digest*, a past honorary chancellor of the National Federation of State Poetry Societies, and current special assistant to the President of Ohio University, where he also teaches ethics and writing. Before relocating to Ohio in 1986, he taught journalism for eight years at Oklahoma State University and advised the campus newspaper. In 1978, at age 26, he was one of the youngest state editors in the history of United Press International. He is married to Diane Sears-Bugeja, a photographer, and lives in Athens, Ohio, with their two children.

This first English language edition of *Millennium's End* was printed for Archer Books in 1999 by Thomson-Shore, Inc. Typefaces are ITC Oficina Serif and ITC Oficina Sans, designed by Erik Spiekemann and his team at MetaDesign.

Book and jacket designed, composed and set by John Taylor-Convery at JTC Imagineering.